CALLED TO FAITH

An Illustrative Journey

CALLED TO FAITH

An Illustrative Journey

JEFF
MERLE

Illustrations by
VIKTORIIA BODNARIUK

Voce Publishing LLC, 2025

vocehouse.com

vocehouse.com

Called To Faith: An Illustrative Journey

Unless otherwise noted, all Bible scripture is taken from the KING JAMES VERSION (KJV), "public domain".

Cover art and Book design by Viktoriia Bodnariuk

First Edition: 2025. Published by Voce Publishing LLC, Minneapolis, MN
Printed in the USA

Library of Congress Control Number:
2026933399

ISBN 979-8-9936492-5-2 (paperback) | ISBN 979-8-9936492-7-6 (hardcover)

ISBN 979-8-9936492-9-0 (large print hardcover)

ISBN 979-8-9936492-0-7 (ebook) | ISBN 979-8-9936492-1-4 (audiobook)

10 9 8 7 6 5 4 3 2 1

Beloved, when I gave all diligence to write unto you of the common salvation, it was needful for me to write unto you, and exhort you that ye should earnestly contend for the faith which was once delivered unto the saints.

✶ *Jude 1:3*

With Gratitude

To my parents, whose prayers for my calling to faith are answered.

To Viktoriia, my business partner and project collaborator, for her God given talent as an artist and illustrator in providing beautiful illustrations of the scripture, story and message herein.

Table of Contents

Preface

This book is about God, and faith in him, from the very beginning. You won't find commentary or opinion, mine or anyone else's. It's an expository of scripture, so his word is the story unfolding, it's truth be told. What's written in telling the story outside from quoted scripture is sound doctrine. Beautiful illustrations provide the reader with visual references of scripture. It's not an exhaustive presentation of figures of faith and events, but of many, by whom and whereby the intent of the writing is met.

I thank God for its writing. And to readers of it, my prayer is that it opens him up to you, as the scripture and its understanding has for me.

Being called to faith has changed my life forever. May you also be called to faith and may it do the same for you.

God Bless!

Introduction

To all readers of this book, may you experience the love of God, and understand his desire is to save as many as who come to him.

But as many as received him, to them gave he power to become the sons of God, even to them that believe on his name:

✳ *John 1:12*

What is Faith?

Faith is belief in God and his word.

But without faith it is impossible to please him: for he that cometh to God must believe that he is, and that he is a rewarder of them that diligently seek him.

✳ *Hebrews 11:6*

Now faith is the substance of things hoped for, the evidence of things not seen. For by it the elders obtained a good report. Through faith we understand that the worlds were framed by the word of God, so that things which are seen were not made of things which do appear.

✳ *Hebrews 11:1-3*

So then faith cometh by hearing, and hearing by the word of God.

✳ *Romans 10:17*

Faith is part of God's protection, his armor we wear.

Above all, taking the shield of faith, wherewith ye shall be able to quench all the fiery darts of the wicked.

✳ *Ephesians 6:16*

This book is an intro to the faith, starting at the beginning of Biblical and human history, and exposing scripture and several figures of faith in both the Old and New Testaments, whom God chose to sow his word among his people, among nations, among Jew and Gentile alike.

Old Testament prophecies on Jesus' life, death and resurrection, all of which were fulfilled, together number in the hundreds, and he is referred to, albeit in different ways, in every book of the Bible. This foretelling of him is a testament to God's overarching will, redemption offered in Christ, his work on our behalf, our sin debt purchased with his own life, securing deliverance from the bondage and condemnation of sin for those who are saved in him.

We either come to and follow Christ and be part of his Kingdom, or we follow the world and a self-directed path. The Apostle Paul writes;

That if thou shalt confess with thy mouth the Lord Jesus, and shalt believe in thine heart that God hath raised him from the dead, thou shalt be saved. For with the heart man believeth unto righteousness; and with the mouth confession is made unto salvation.

✳ *Romans 10:9-10*

Paul writes God has predestined those to be conformed to Christ's image, that he calls us to fellowship with Jesus.

For whom he did foreknow, he also did predestinate to be conformed to the image of his Son, that he might be the firstborn among many brethren. Moreover whom he did predestinate, them he also called: and whom he called, them he also justified: and whom he justified, them he also glorified.

✳ *Romans 8:29-30*

God is faithful, by whom ye were called unto the fellowship of his Son Jesus Christ our Lord.

✳ *1 Corinthians 1:9*

And he writes that God chose us in him, adopting us for

sonship, before we even existed, that he foreknew those who would be his.

According as he hath chosen us in him before the foundation of the world, that we should be holy and without blame before him in love: Having predestinated us unto the adoption of children by Jesus Christ to himself, according to the good pleasure of his will,

✳ *Ephesians 1:4-5*

In whom also we have obtained an inheritance, being predestinated according to the purpose of him who worketh all things after the counsel of his own will:

✳ *Ephesians 1:11*

And Peter writes that God had foreknowledge of his elect, that he knew who would be saved by Christ.

Elect according to the foreknowledge of God the Father, through sanctification of the Spirit, unto obedience and sprinkling of the blood of Jesus Christ: Grace unto you, and peace, be multiplied.

✳ *1 Peter 1:2*

If you have a desire to learn more about God and his son Jesus, the light of the world, through whom exists the only path to your salvation, believe in and follow Jesus, make him your Lord and Savior, and be saved in him by the glory and grace of him who sent him.

We are created in God's image, with an eternal soul. When we die, we face him.

And as it is appointed unto men once to die, but after this the judgment:

✳ *Hebrews 9:27*

In accepting Jesus as our Lord and Savior and following him, we are given the gift of eternal life.

My sheep hear my voice, and I know them, and they follow me: And I give unto them eternal life; and they shall never perish, neither shall any man pluck them out of my hand.

✳ *John 10:27-28*

Or, for non-believers, those who reject him, they will face God's wrath.

He that believeth on the Son hath everlasting life: and he that believeth not the Son shall not see life; but the wrath of God abideth on him.

✳ *John 3:36*

Jesus makes it clear he came to separate his followers from those who choose the world and its ways over him.

Suppose ye that I am come to give peace on earth? I tell you, Nay; but rather division:

✳ *Luke 12:51*

Enter ye in at the strait gate: for wide is the gate, and broad is the way, that leadeth to destruction, and many there be which go in thereat: Because strait is the gate, and narrow is the way, which leadeth unto life, and few there be that find it.

✳ *Mathew 7:13-14*

It is our hope this book can provide insight for the purpose of leading you to follow Christ, to start your journey of faith, and to let God's desire to save you draw you to him, to salvation, to an eternity with him beginning right now in this life. You are not guaranteed tomorrow, so come to Christ while you still have time. What a gift it is to be part of his kingdom now and forever.

I. God: Father, Son, Holy Spirit

There is only one God. He is Triune, existing eternally as three distinct, coequal and coeternal persons, God the Father, God the Son (Jesus), and God the Holy Spirit. He is the only true and living God. He is creator of the universe and everything in it, and is sovereign over all. He is all powerful, all knowing, always truthful, always present, never changing. It's his characteristics that give us faith in his will for our lives, we trust in him and his word as truth.

And God said unto Moses, I AM THAT I AM: and he said, Thus shalt thou say unto the children of Israel, I AM hath sent me unto you.

✳ *Exodus 3:14*

A Prayer of Moses the Man of God

Before the mountains were brought forth, or ever thou hadst formed the earth and the world, even from everlasting to everlasting, thou art God.

✳ *Psalm 90:2*

For thus saith the high and lofty One that inhabiteth eternity, whose name is Holy; I dwell in the high and holy place, with him also that is of a contrite and humble spirit, to revive the spirit of the humble, and to revive the heart of the contrite ones.

✳ *Isaiah 57:15*

Your father Abraham rejoiced to see my day: and he saw it, and was glad. Then said the Jews unto him, Thou art not yet fifty years old, and hast thou seen Abraham? Jesus said unto them, Verily, verily, I say unto you, Before Abraham was, I am.

✳ *John 8:58*

And Jesus came and spake unto them, saying, All power is given unto me in heaven and in earth.

✳ *Mathew 28:18*

I am Alpha and Omega, the beginning and the ending, saith the Lord, which is, and which was, and which is to come, the Almighty.

✳ *Revelation 1:8*

In the Beginning

II. The Creation

In the beginning God created the heaven and the earth.

✳ *Genesis 1:1*

So God created man in his own image, in the image of God created he him; male and female created he them.

✳ *Genesis 1:27*

And the LORD God formed man of the dust of the ground, and breathed into his nostrils the breath of life; and man became a living soul.

✳ *Genesis 2:7*

And the rib, which the LORD God had taken from man, made he a woman, and brought her unto the man.

✳ *Genesis 2:22*

John writes; *Through him all things were made; without him nothing was made that has been made.*

✳ *John 1:3*

Paul writes: *For the invisible things of him from the creation of the world are clearly seen, being understood by the things that are made, even his eternal power and Godhead; so that they are without excuse:*

✳ *Romans 1:20*

III. Fall of Man

History begins with God's creation of everything, man in his image, with an eternal soul. Man started in harmony with God. Adam and Eve, in the Garden of Eden, there by God's direct, were instructed by him they could eat from any tree in the garden except the tree of the knowledge of good and evil.

From a Serpent, the enemy of God, Satan, talked to Eve, and tempted and deceived her. She ate fruit from the tree she was instructed by God not to eat of, giving to Adam which he ate as well.

This was original sin, the breaking of the creator and creature covenant, or covenant of works God had made with them in instructing them. They became aware of their nakedness, and were ashamed.

God performed the first sacrifice, the shedding of innocent blood as atonement for their sin, and made them animal skins to cover their nakedness. This was a foreshadowing of Christ's death on the cross, the shedding of his innocent blood as atonement for all sin.

The original sin of Adam and Eve was the fall of man, the reason from birth we are all sinners by nature, and must find salvation through Christ, the only way we are justified, made right with God.

David writes; *Behold, I was shapen in iniquity; and in sin did my mother conceive me.*

✶ *Psalm 53:5*

Paul writes; *Wherefore, as by one man sin entered into the world, and death by sin; and so death passed upon all men, for that all have sinned:*

✶ *Romans 5:12*

God gave punishments for this original sin to all involved. The serpent was cursed by God for all its days, to move about amidst the dust on the ground. And God's curse on Satan;

And I will put enmity between thee and the woman, and between thy seed and her seed; it shall bruise thy head, and thou shalt bruise his heel.

✶ *Genesis 3:15*

Enmity refers to the assault waged by Satan against those from the seed of the woman. Thy seed refers to his seed, the reprobate of humanity, followers of self, of him. Her seed, offspring from the woman, from Eve, are those saved in Christ, and Jesus himself, born of the virgin birth, who delivers the fatal blow. Bruise thy head refers to the fatal blow, the complete defeat of Satan, evil and death by Christs' death on the cross and resurrection. Sin and death were conquered, the full debt for sin paid, and sinners reconciled to God. Bruise the heal refers to Christ's suffering on the cross, a temporary, painful but not fatal assault inflicted by Satan.

So in Genesis 3:15 is also the first prophecy and Gospel message in scripture, salvation for the seed of Eve. In the midst of the curse, hope appears, regeneration, God's mercy and grace.

God's punishment for woman is pain in childbirth, and a broken relationship between the sexes, the woman desires the headship role of the man, a desire to control man, but the man will in turn dominate excessively.

God's punishment for man is the cursed ground. He must struggle to produce his food from it, and will ultimately return in death to its dust, from which he was made.

God says to Adam; *In the sweat of thy face shalt thou eat bread, till thou return unto the ground; for out of it wast thou taken: for dust thou art, and unto dust shalt thou return.*

✳ *Genesis 3:19*

IV. The Bible

The Bible is the infallible word of God, inspired and authored by the Holy Spirit through approximately 40 human writers over a period of 1500 years. There are 66 total books (39 Old Testament and 27 New Testament) that together tell a consistent and continuous narrative.

The Old and New Testaments are inextricably and undeniably linked. They are God's revealing of himself and his plan for all of humanity, primarily to Israel as a nation being built in the Old Testament, to Abraham, Isaac and Jacob, its forefathers, and to prophets, Kings and other individuals of faith.

Prophecies throughout the Old Testament foretell of the Messiah, and to salvation offered through him. In the New Testament, Jesus' life, message, death, and resurrection are recorded, the prophecies of the Old Testament regarding the new covenant in him being fulfilled.

Forgiveness of sin for salvation has always been under grace and by faith, from Christ's work on the cross. In the Old Testament, for those faithful to God, this applied ahead to them. And like for us now under the New Covenant, the penalty for sin has been paid once and for all, satisfying God as Judge.

Therefore it is of faith, that it might be by grace; to the end the promise might be sure to all the seed; not to that only which is of the law, but to that also which is of the faith of Abraham; who is the father of us all,

✳ *Romans 4:16*

Ongoing confession of our sins to God is part of our sanctification. This is not works, and not a requirement for salvation. Ongoing confession and repentance gives God glory, satisfying him as Heavenly Father.

If we confess our sins, he is faithful and just to forgive us our sins, and to cleanse us from all unrighteousness.

✳ *1 John 1:9*

Judicial forgiveness is for salvation. Paternal forgiveness for ongoing cleansing.

God required ritualistic sacrifice for ongoing cleansing of sin in the Old Testament. This practice is no longer required under the New Covenant.

Jesus says in Mathew 22:20; *This cup is the new testament in my blood, which is shed for you.*

In this scripture Jesus initiates the New Covenant at the Last Supper, the completion of the covenant happening over the following days with his death and resurrection.

The prophecy in the book of Jeremiah is fulfilled, and also quoted as such in Hebrews. This new covenant between God and his elect replaces the Mosaic one he'd made with Israel during the Exodus.

Behold, the days come, saith the LORD, that I will make a new covenant with the house of Israel, and with the house of Judah: Not according to the covenant that I made with their fathers in the day that I took them by the hand to bring them out of the land of Egypt; which my covenant they brake, although I was an husband unto them, saith the LORD: But this shall be the covenant that I will make with the house of Israel; After those days, saith the LORD, I will put my law in their inward parts, and write it in their hearts; and will be their God, and they shall be my people. And they shall teach no more every man his neighbour, and every man his brother, saying, Know the LORD: for they shall all know me, from the least of them unto the greatest of them, saith the LORD: for I will forgive their iniquity, and I will remember their sin no more.

* *Jeremiah 31:31-34*

And in several chapters of the Bible scripture reveals the final events of mankind, Christ's return and God's new kingdom that will replace the current Heaven and Earth.

Old Testament: Called to Faith

God worked through the lives of many faithful followers in the Old Testament. He revealed himself as sovereign, established his law and made covenants with them to carry out his plan to build a nation. And he through them laid the groundwork for his plan for all of mankind, with Christ's foretelling throughout.

V. Abel

Genesis 4 tells of Cain and Abel, sons of Adam and Eve. Abel, a Shepherd, is younger brother to Cain a farmer. Both offered sacrifices to God, Cane some of his harvest, Abel a firstborn lamb from his flock. God was pleased with Abel's offering but not Cain's.

By faith Abel offered unto God a more excellent sacrifice than Cain, by which he obtained witness that he was righteous, God testifying of his gifts: and by it he being dead yet speaketh.

✲ *Hebrews 11:4*

Abel's sacrifice signifies an act of faith in God, Cain's an act of self. Cane kills Abel from jealousy and envy, lies to God and is insolent.

And the LORD said unto Cain, Where is Abel thy brother? And he said, I know not: Am I my brother's keeper?

✲ *Genesis 4:9*

Cane is exiled by God, and marked not to be killed, an act of both punishment and mercy.

And Cain said unto the LORD, My punishment is greater than I can bear. Behold, thou hast driven me out this day from the face of the earth; and from thy face shall I be hid; and I shall be a fugitive and a vagabond in the earth; and it shall come to pass, that every one that findeth me shall slay me. And the LORD said unto him, Therefore whosoever slayeth Cain, vengeance shall be taken on him sevenfold. And the LORD set a mark upon Cain, lest any finding him should kill him. And Cain went out from the presence of the LORD, and dwelt in the land of Nod, on the east of Eden.

✻ *Genesis 4:13*

Abel's faith in God and the righteousness of his actions are mentioned in New Testament scripture in both the book of Luke and aforementioned Hebrews.

From the blood of Abel unto the blood of Zacharias, which perished between the altar and the temple: verily I say unto you, It shall be required of this generation.

✻ *Luke 11:5*

VI. Noah

God chose Noah, a faithful and righteous servant, and warned him of a Flood that would destroy the Earth and its wicked inhabitants. He instructed him to build an Ark and gather his family, and also male and female pairs of all living things whereby after the Flood they would repopulate the Earth.

And God said unto Noah, The end of all flesh is come before me; for the earth is filled with violence through them; and, behold, I will destroy them with the earth."

✻ *Genesis 6:13*

And the dove came in to him in the evening; and, lo, in her mouth was an olive leaf plucked off: so Noah knew that the waters were abated from off the earth.

✻ *Genesis 8:11*

By faith Noah, being warned of God of things not seen as yet, moved with fear, prepared an ark to the saving of his house; by the which he condemned the world, and became heir of the righteousness which is by faith.

✻ *Hebrews 11:7*

VII. Abraham

God called on Abram (later Abraham) to leave his family and homeland to establish a new nation and people in the land of Caanan, promising to bless him and his descendants.

Now the LORD had said unto Abram, Get thee out of thy country, and from thy kindred, and from thy father's house, unto a land that I will shew thee: And I will make of thee a great nation, and I will bless thee, and make thy name great; and thou shalt be a blessing: And I will bless them that bless thee, and curse him that curseth thee: and in thee shall all families of the earth be blessed.

✳ *Genesis 12:1-3*

Abraham, his wife Sarah and Nephew Lot travel to Egypt due to famine, but there they encounter trouble with the Pharoah.

Abraham warns Sarah that because she is attractive, she will be desired and he could be killed if they knew she was his wife, so he lies to Pharoah saying Sarah is his sister. She is indeed desired as he'd warned and she is asked into Pharoah's household. As a result, for their pursuit of her, Pharoah is plagued by the Lord, he eventually realizes that Sarah is Abraham's wife, the reason for the plagues, and so tells them to leave Egypt.

And the LORD plagued Pharaoh and his house with great plagues because of Sarai Abram's wife. And Pharaoh called Abram, and

said, What is this that thou hast done unto me? Why didst thou not tell me that she was thy wife? Why saidst thou, She is my sister? So I might have taken her to me to wife: now therefore behold thy wife, take her, and go thy way. And Pharaoh commanded his men concerning him: and they sent him away, and his wife, and all that he had.

✴ *Genesis 12:17-20*

God tells Abraham his descendants will be captive for 400 years, and then be set free.

And he said unto Abram, Know of a surety that thy seed shall be a stranger in a land that is not theirs, and shall serve them; and they shall afflict them four hundred years; And also that nation, whom they shall serve, will I judge: and afterward shall they come out with great substance.

✴ *Genesis 15:13-14*

And the Lord said to Abraham:

As for me, behold, my covenant is with thee, and thou shalt be a father of many nations. Neither shall thy name any more be called Abram, but thy name shall be Abraham; for a father of many nations have I made thee.

✴ *Genesis 17:4-5*

God appeared to Abraham at Mamre, as three men, and told him again he would have a son with Sarah.

And they said unto him, Where is Sarah thy wife? And he said, Behold, in the tent. And he said, I will certainly return unto thee according to the time of life; and, lo, Sarah thy wife shall have a son. And Sarah heard it in the tent door, which was behind him. Now Abraham and Sarah were old and well stricken in age; and it ceased to be with Sarah after the manner of women. Therefore Sarah laughed within herself, saying, After I am waxed old shall I have pleasure, my lord being old also? And the LORD said unto Abraham, Wherefore did Sarah laugh, saying, Shall I of a surety bear a child, which am old? Is any thing too hard for the LORD? At the time appointed I will return unto thee, according to the time of life, and Sarah shall have a son. Then Sarah denied, saying, I laughed not; for she was afraid. And he said, Nay; but thou didst laugh.

✳ *Genesis 18:9-15*

Abraham's son was born shortly thereafter, in the next year, he being 100 and Sarah 90 years old. God told them to name him Isaac, meaning laughter, because Sarah had laughed.

God tested Abraham's faith by telling him to take his son Isaac and offer him as a burnt offering upon a mountain in Moriah.

And the angel of the LORD called unto him out of heaven, and said, Abraham, Abraham: and he said, Here am I. And he said, Lay not thine hand upon the lad, neither do thou any thing unto him: for now I know that thou fearest God, seeing thou hast not withheld thy son, thine only son from me. And Abraham lifted up his eyes, and looked, and behold behind him a ram caught in a thicket by his horns: and Abraham went and took the ram, and offered him up for a burnt offering in the stead of his son.

✳ *Genesis 22:11-13*

God tells Abraham again his seed will be a source of blessing for all nations. God fulfills this promise with Christ as Messiah being born of his seed, his descendants in the tribe of Judah.

And the angel of the LORD called unto Abraham out of heaven the second time, And said, By myself have I sworn, saith the LORD, for because thou hast done this thing, and hast not withheld thy son, thine only son: That in blessing I will bless thee, and in multiplying I will multiply thy seed as the stars of the heaven, and as the sand which is upon the sea shore; and thy seed shall possess the gate of his enemies; And in thy seed shall all the nations of the earth be blessed; because thou hast obeyed my voice.

✳ *Genesis 22:15-18*

Abraham had faith in God, listened to and obeyed his commands.

By faith Abraham, when he was called to go out into a place which

he should after receive for an inheritance, obeyed; and he went out, not knowing whither he went. By faith he sojourned in the land of promise, as in a strange country, dwelling in tabernacles with Isaac and Jacob, the heirs with him of the same promise: For he looked for a city which hath foundations, whose builder and maker is God.

＊ *Hebrews 11:8-10*

And Abraham gave all that he had unto Isaac.

＊ *Genesis 25:5*

And these are the days of the years of Abraham's life which he lived, an hundred threescore and fifteen years. Then Abraham gave up the ghost, and died in a good old age, an old man, and full of years; and was gathered to his people.

＊ *Genesis 25:7-8*

VIII. Isaac

Abraham sent his servant to his homeland to find a wife for his son Isaac, he didn't want him marrying a Canaanite. In Mesopotamia, in the city of Nahor, the servant waited by a well with the ten camels he'd brought with him, where the women draw water in the evenings. He prayed to the Lord to let the woman who showed kindness by providing water from her pitcher so he and the camels could drink be the one God picked for Isaac to marry.

And it came to pass, before he had done speaking, that, behold, Rebekah came out, who was born to Bethuel, son of Milcah, the wife of Nahor, Abraham's brother, with her pitcher upon her shoulder. And the damsel was very fair to look upon, a virgin, neither had any man known her: and she went down to the well, and filled her pitcher, and came up. And the servant ran to meet her, and said, Let me, I pray thee, drink a little water of thy pitcher. And she said, Drink, my lord: and she hasted, and let down her pitcher upon her hand, and gave him drink. And when she had done giving him drink, she said, I will draw water for thy camels also, until they have done drinking.

✳ *Genesis 24:15-19*

Abraham's servant explained to her family of his prayers to the Lord for finding a chosen wife for Isaac. And they learned Isaac was son of her father's brother, and of his prosperity

and blessings in life from God. Rebekah agreed to return with Abraham's servant and her family blessed her as she left.

And they called Rebekah, and said unto her, Wilt thou go with this man? And she said, I will go. And they sent away Rebekah their sister, and her nurse, and Abraham's servant, and his men. And they blessed Rebekah, and said unto her, Thou art our sister, be thou the mother of thousands of millions, and let thy secd possess the gate of those which hate them.

✳ *Genesis 24:58-60*

Isaac see's the camels approaching and walks toward them.

And Rebekah lifted up her eyes, and when she saw Isaac, she lighted off the camel. For she had said unto the servant, What man is this that walketh in the field to meet us? And the servant had said, It is my master: therefore she took a veil, and covered herself. And the servant told Isaac all things that he had done. And Isaac brought her into his mother Sarah's tent, and took Rebekah, and she became his wife; and he loved her: and Isaac was comforted after his mother's death.

✳ *Genesis 24:64-67*

Isaac and Rebekah had twin sons. And she enquired of God why the two struggled within her.

And the LORD said unto her, Two nations are in thy womb, and two manner of people shall be separated from thy bowels; and the one people shall be stronger than the other people; and the elder shall serve the younger.

✳ *Genesis 25:23*

God told Isaac not to go to Egypt, but to dwell in the land he would tell him of, that he would bless he and his seed, that many countries would be had, and that he would fulfill the promises he'd made to Abraham.

And the LORD appeared unto him, and said, Go not down into Egypt; dwell in the land which I shall tell thee of: Sojourn in this land, and I will be with thee, and will bless thee; for unto thee, and unto thy seed, I will give all these countries, and I will perform the oath which I sware unto Abraham thy father; And I will make thy seed to multiply as the stars of heaven, and will give unto thy seed all these countries; and in thy seed shall all the nations of the earth be blessed; Because that Abraham obeyed my voice, and kept my charge, my commandments, my statutes, and my laws. And Isaac dwelt in Gerar:

✳ *Genesis 26:2-6*

Then Isaac sowed in that land, and received in the same year an hundredfold: and the LORD blessed him. And the man waxed great, and went forward, and grew until he became very great: For he had possession of flocks, and possession of herds, and great store of servants: and the Philistines envied him.

✳ *Genesis 26:12-14*

Because of Isaacs prosperity, he was told by King Abimelech to depart the land.

And Abimelech said unto Isaac, Go from us; for thou art much mightier than we. And Isaac departed thence, and pitched his tent in the valley of Gerar, and dwelt there.

✳ *Genesis 26:16-17*

Later in years, when Isaac was old, Jacob, following along with Rebekah's plan, tricks Isaac into giving him the blessing, which by birthright was to go to his twin brother Esau, who was born first.

And his father Isaac said unto him, Come near now, and kiss me, my son. And he came near, and kissed him: and he smelled the smell of his raiment, and blessed him, and said, See, the smell of my son is as the smell of a field which the LORD hath blessed: Therefore God give thee of the dew of heaven, and the fatness of the earth, and plenty of corn and wine: Let people serve thee, and nations bow down to thee: be lord over thy brethren, and let thy mother's sons bow down to thee: cursed be every one that curseth thee, and blessed be he that blesseth thee.

✳ *Genesis 27:26-29*

Issac passes amongst his people.

And Jacob came unto Isaac his father unto Mamre, unto the city of Arbah, which is Hebron, where Abraham and Isaac sojourned. And the days of Isaac were an hundred and fourscore years. And Isaac gave up the ghost, and died, and was gathered unto his people, being old and full of days: and his sons Esau and Jacob buried him.

✳ *Genesis 35:27-29*

IX. Jacob

When Jacob learned of his brother Esau's plan to kill him for stealing the birthright blessing, Rebekah urged him to leave town. Isaac also did not want him marrying a Canaanite, so he'd been told to go and stay with his uncle Laban, Rebekah's brother. En route, he stopped to rest at Luz.

And he dreamed, and behold a ladder set up on the earth, and the top of it reached to heaven: and behold the angels of God ascending and descending on it. And, behold, the LORD stood above it, and said, I am the LORD God of Abraham thy father, and the God of Isaac: the land whereon thou liest, to thee will I give it, and to thy seed; And thy seed shall be as the dust of the earth, and thou shalt spread abroad to the west, and to the east, and to the north, and to the south: and in thee and in thy seed shall all the families of the earth be blessed.

✳ *Genesis 28:12-14*

And Jacob rose up early in the morning, and took the stone that he had put for his pillows, and set it up for a pillar, and poured oil upon the top of it. And he called the name of that place Beth-el: but the name of that city was called Luz at the first. And Jacob vowed a vow, saying, If God will be with me, and will keep me in this way that I go, and will give me bread to eat, and raiment to put on, So that I come again to my father's house in peace; then shall the LORD be my God: And this stone, which I have set for

a pillar, shall be God's house: and of all that thou shalt give me I will surely give the tenth unto thee.

✳ *Genesis 28:18-22*

Jacob arrived in the East, in Haran where Laban lived, and came upon a well with flocks of sheep lying near. He inquired of them there about Laban, during which time Laban's daughter Rachel showed up at the well with sheep.

And it came to pass, when Jacob saw Rachel the daughter of Laban his mother's brother, and the sheep of Laban his mother's brother, that Jacob went near, and rolled the stone from the well's mouth, and watered the flock of Laban his mother's brother. And Jacob kissed Rachel, and lifted up his voice, and wept. And Jacob told Rachel that he was her father's brother, and that he was Rebekah's son: and she ran and told her father.

✳ *Genesis 29:10-12*

And after remaining with Laban for about a month, he asks Jacob to stay and work for him. Jacob agrees to work for him for 7 years, for the right to marry his younger daughter Rachel, but on the wedding night is duped into marrying her sister Leah, Laban promising Rachel after 7 more years. After serving Laban for 20 years, God instructed him to return to his homeland in Canaan.

With his wives and children and many animals he'd acquired during his service to Laban, he left for his homeland.

As Jacob nears home he learns of his Brother Esau's approach with 400 men, and is fearful. That night Jacob wrestles throughout the night with a man who tells him his name is no longer Jacob, but Israel, Jacob realizing the man is God.

And Jacob was left alone; and there wrestled a man with him until the breaking of the day. And when he saw that he prevailed not against him, he touched the hollow of his thigh; and the hollow of Jacob's thigh was out of joint, as he wrestled with him. And he said, Let me go, for the day breaketh. And he said, I will not let thee go, except thou bless me. And he said unto him, What is thy name? And he said, Jacob. And he said, Thy name shall be called no more Jacob, but Israel: for as a prince hast thou power with God and with men, and hast prevailed. And Jacob asked him, and said, Tell me, I pray thee, thy name. And he said, Wherefore is it that thou dost ask after my name? And he blessed him there. And Jacob called the name of the place Peniel: for I have seen God face to face, and my life is preserved.

✳ *Genesis 32:24-30*

The following day's reunion with his brother was peaceful.

Jacob had 12 sons, each becoming one of the family lines known as the 12 Tribes of Israel. They are: Reuben, Simeon, Levi,

Jacob

Judah, Dan, Naphtali, Gad, Asher, Issachar, Zebulun, Joseph, and Benjamin.

Joseph, son to Rachel, went from being enslaved to being put in a leadership position in Egypt.

He was first sold into slavery by his jealous brothers and later imprisoned as a result of false accusations by Potiphar's wife.

While yet imprisoned, he was asked to interpret Pharaoh's dreams regarding the impending famine, and subsequently put in charge of establishing and ensuring food stores for the Egyptians and ultimately his family during these years.

Jacob gave Joseph a parcel of land near a well that in the New Testament is referred to as Jacob's well, its significance being the place where Jesus meets the Samaritan woman there. He reveals himself to her as Christ and offers her living water, whereby she begins spreading the word of him to her people.

En route from Judea to Galilee, Jesus stops in Samaria.

Then cometh he to a city of Samaria, which is called Sychar, near to the parcel of ground that Jacob gave to his son Joseph. Now Jacob's well was there. Jesus therefore, being wearied with his journey, sat thus on the well: and it was about the sixth hour.

There cometh a woman of Samaria to draw water: Jesus saith unto her, Give me to drink.

✷ *John 4:5-7*

In conversation between Jesus and the Samaritan woman;

Art thou greater than our father Jacob, which gave us the well, and drank thereof himself, and his children, and his cattle? Jesus answered and said unto her, Whosoever drinketh of this water shall thirst again: But whosoever drinketh of the water that I shall give him shall never thirst; but the water that I shall give him shall be in him a well of water springing up into everlasting life.

✷ *John 4:12-14*

And through Judah (Jacob's son with Leah), is the lineage of both David and Jesus.

Like the lives of Abraham and Isaac, Jacob's life exemplified both hardship and many blessings from God. They are considered the forefathers of Israel, being faithful to and obeying God's direction, the covenant he made with them to build and prosper Israel as a nation from their descendants.

X. **Moses**

Moses was found by Pharaoh's daughter at 3 months old floating in a basket among the Reeds of the Nile River where she bathed. He was placed there by his mother, with intent to save him from Pharaoh's decree to kill all Hebrew newborn boys in fear of the growing Israelite population. She adopted him and he spent his youth in Egyptian royalty.

It is written; *And the daughter of Pharaoh came down to wash herself at the river; and her maidens walked along by the river's side; and when she saw the ark among the flags, she sent her maid to fetch it. And when she had opened it, she saw the child: and, behold, the babe wept. And she had compassion on him, and said, This is one of the Hebrews' children. Then said his sister to Pharaoh's daughter, Shall I go and call to thee a nurse of the Hebrew women, that she may nurse the child for thee? And Pharaoh's daughter said to her, Go. And the maid went and called the child's mother. And Pharaoh's daughter said unto her, Take this child away, and nurse it for me, and I will give thee thy wages. And the woman took the child, and nursed it. And the child grew, and she brought him unto Pharaoh's daughter, and he became her son. And she called his name Moses: and she said, Because I drew him out of the water.*

✳ *Exodus 2:5-10*

God's providence, orchestration and protection of Moses

from Pharaoh's decree is evident in his being saved. Moses calling from God came later in life.

By faith Moses, when he was come to years, refused to be called the son of Pharaoh's daughter; Choosing rather to suffer affliction with the people of God, than to enjoy the pleasures of sin for a season; Esteeming the reproach of Christ greater riches than the treasures in Egypt: for he had respect unto the recompence of the reward. By faith he forsook Egypt, not fearing the wrath of the king: for he endured, as seeing him who is invisible. Through faith he kept the passover, and the sprinkling of blood, lest he that destroyed the firstborn should touch them.

* *Hebrews 11:24-28*

Moses spent 40 years hiding in the desert for killing an Egyptian. God revealed himself and called on him through the burning bush, telling him to lead the Israelites out of captivity in Egypt, and sending him to confront Pharaoh, whose insolence to God brought the wrath of plagues on the Egyptians. Following God's wrath, Moses leads them out of Egypt, departing the Red Sea to escape pursuit by Pharaoh's Army, whom God destroyed with its walls of water once the Israelites were safe.

Moses received the 10 commandments from God on Mount Sinai and shortly thereafter, God spoke them directly to the Israelites. They spent the next 40 years wandering in the

desert, being provided for and kept safe by God until under his direct, Moses appointed Joshua to lead them across the Jordan River into the land God had promised them. Moses died in the desert, never reaching the promised land himself, as punishment from God for an earlier act of disobedience.

And the LORD said unto Moses, Depart, and go up hence, thou and the people which thou hast brought up out of the land of Egypt, unto the land which I sware unto Abraham, to Isaac, and to Jacob, saying, Unto thy seed will I give it: And I will send an angel before thee; and I will drive out the Canaanite, the Amorite, and the Hittite, and the Perizzite, the Hivite, and the Jebusite: Unto a land flowing with milk and honey: for I will not go up in the midst of thee; for thou art a stiffnecked people: lest I consume thee in the way.

✳ *Exodus 33:1-3*

XI. David

Because of King Saul's disobedience, God called on the prophet Samuel to find his replacement, to anoint a new King of the Israelites. Samuel went to Jesse's home, and when David was presented last among his many sons, God chose him, because of his heart for God.

Again, Jesse made seven of his sons to pass before Samuel. And Samuel said unto Jesse, The LORD hath not chosen these. And Samuel said unto Jesse, Are here all thy children? And he said, There remaineth yet the youngest, and, behold, he keepeth the sheep. And Samuel said unto Jesse, Send and fetch him: for we will not sit down till he come hither. And he sent, and brought him in. Now he was ruddy, and withal of a beautiful countenance, and goodly to look to. And the LORD said, Arise, anoint him: for this is he.

✳ *1 Samuel 16:10-12*

And when he had removed him, he raised up unto them David to be their king; to whom also he gave testimony, and said, I have found David the son of Jesse, a man after mine own heart, which shall fulfil all my will.

✳ *Acts 13:22*

David is considered Israel's greatest King. After his anointing, many events in his life reflected his faith, devotion and service to God. From shepherding his family's flock, he was called to work for King Saul.

David slayed Goliath as a youth, a giant in the Philistine army, who David viewed had affronted the armies of the living God, Goliath taunting them to bring forth a worthy adversary for single combat.

And it came to pass, when the Philistine arose, and came and drew nigh to meet David, that David hasted, and ran toward the army to meet the Philistine. And David put his hand in his bag, and took thence a stone, and slang it, and smote the Philistine in his forehead, that the stone sunk into his forehead; and he fell upon his face to the earth. So David prevailed over the Philistine with a sling and with a stone, and smote the Philistine, and slew him; but there was no sword in the hand of David.

✳ *1 Samuel 17:48-50*

Having seen the popularity among the Israelites David was gaining as a result of his defeating Goliath, Saul grew increasingly jealous of him and set forth to kill him. David fled and spent years on the run, hiding from Saul and his men to avoid being killed. Upon Saul's death, David took the throne. While King, he put his faith in God and was blessed, but made grave mistakes in tandem, even taking Uriah's wife Bathsheba for himself and having him moved to the front lines in battle where he was killed.

David had a desire to properly house the Ark of the Covenant, the symbol of God's presence and covenant with the Israelites, so he was heartfelt to build a temple for the Lord.

Now it came to pass, as David sat in his house, that David said to Nathan the prophet, Lo, I dwell in an house of cedars, but the ark of the covenant of the LORD remaineth under curtains.

✱ *1 Chronicles 17:1*

However, God intended for his son Solomon to build it.

Go and tell David my servant, Thus saith the LORD, Thou shalt not build me an house to dwell in:

✱ *1 Chronicles 17:4*

And it shall come to pass, when thy days be expired that thou must go to be with thy fathers, that I will raise up thy seed after thee, which shall be of thy sons; and I will establish his kingdom. He shall build me an house, and I will stablish his throne for ever. I will be his father, and he shall be my son: and I will not take my mercy away from him, as I took it from him that was before thee: But I will settle him in mine house and in my kingdom for ever: and his throne shall be established for evermore.

✱ *1 Chronicles 17:11-14*

David

This type of scripture like many others in the Bible is typology, it having immediate meaning for its original context, but also foreshadowing a future, complete fulfillment. In this passage, the immediate fulfillment is the Davidic Covenant, God's promise to David through the prophet Nathan, for his and his descendants kingship in Israel, beginning with him and Solomon, and for Solomon's building of the temple.

And in the duality of the passage, its second and complete meaning, the foreshadowing of Christ's ultimate and eternal reign.

David amassed precious metals and other materials in victories over other nations and he dedicated these to the Lord, and Solomon later used the materials for pillars and other building components.

And David took the shields of gold that were on the servants of Hadarezer, and brought them to Jerusalem. Likewise from Tibhath, and from Chun, cities of Hadarezer, brought David very much brass, wherewith Solomon made the brasen sea, and the pillars, and the vessels of brass.

* *1 Chronicles 18:7-8*

David wrote nearly half of the 150 Psalms in the Old Testament Book of Psalm, and prophesied Christ's coming a thousand years prior to his arrival in one of the most quoted of the

Psalms, of Old Testament scripture in the New Testament.

The LORD said unto my Lord, Sit thou at my right hand, until I make thine enemies thy footstool. The LORD shall send the rod of thy strength out of Zion: rule thou in the midst of thine enemies. Thy people shall be willing in the day of thy power, in the beauties of holiness from the womb of the morning: thou hast the dew of thy youth. The LORD hath sworn, and will not repent, Thou art a priest for ever after the order of Melchizedek. The Lord at thy right hand shall strike through kings in the day of his wrath. He shall judge among the heathen, he shall fill the places with the dead bodies; he shall wound the heads over many countries. He shall drink of the brook in the way: therefore shall he lift up the head.

✳ *Psalm 110*

Christ is Foretold

XII. Prophecy of the Coming Messiah

The Old Testament has many mentions of the coming Messiah.

Therefore the Lord himself shall give you a sign; Behold, a virgin shall conceive, and bear a son, and shall call his name Immanuel.

✳ *Isaiah 7:14*

For unto us a child is born, unto us a son is given: and the government shall he upon his shoulder: and his name shall be called Wonderful, Counsellor, The mighty God, The everlasting Father, The Prince of Peace. Of the increase of his government and peace there shall be no end, upon the throne of David, and upon his kingdom, to order it, and to establish it with judgment and with justice from henceforth even for ever. The zeal of the LORD of hosts will perform this.

✳ *Isaiah 9:6-7*

But thou, Beth-lehem Ephratah, though thou be little among the thousands of Judah, yet out of thee shall he come forth unto me that is to be ruler in Israel; whose goings forth have been from of old, from everlasting.

✳ *Micah 5:2*

XIII. A Plan of Salvation

Isaiah prophesied Christ's death for the forgiveness of our sins, our redemption in him.

But he was wounded for our transgressions, he was bruised for our iniquities: the chastisement of our peace was upon him; and with his stripes we are healed.

✳ *Isaiah 53:5*

The Apostle Paul writes of God's redemptive plan of salvation, accomplished in Jesus Christ;

And without controversy great is the mystery of godliness: God was manifest in the flesh, justified in the spirit, seen by angels, preached unto the Gentiles, believed on in the world, received up into glory.

✳ *1 Timothy 3:16*

XIV. John the Baptist

Old Testament Prophesies on the coming of the Messiah were many, also prophesied was of one who would come before Jesus, to pave the way for him. John the Baptist was chosen by God to spread the word among the people of the coming Messiah, prior to Jesus beginning his ministry, and prior to the New Covenant of his death, resurrection and ascension.

There was a man sent from God, whose name was John. The same came for a witness, to bear witness of the Light, that all men through him might believe. He was not that Light, but was sent to bear witness of that Light.

✳ *John 1:6-8*

The voice of him that crieth in the wilderness, Prepare ye the way of the LORD, make straight in the desert a highway for our God.

✳ *Isaiah 40:3*

Behold, I will send my messenger, and he shall prepare the way before me: and the Lord, whom ye seek, shall suddenly come to his temple, even the messenger of the covenant, whom ye delight in: behold, he shall come, saith the LORD of hosts.

✳ *Malachi 3:1*

Mathew mentions Isaiah's prophecy so indeed we know it is in reference to John the Baptist.

In those days came John the Baptist, preaching in the wilderness of Judaea, And saying, Repent ye: for the kingdom of heaven is at hand. For this is he that was spoken of by the prophet Esaias, saying, The voice of one crying in the wilderness, Prepare ye the way of the Lord, make his paths straight.

✳ *Mathew 3:1-3*

And Jesus himself recognizes John the Baptist as subject in this Old Testament scripture, as written by Mathew.

For this is he, of whom it is written, Behold, I send my messenger before thy face, which shall prepare thy way before thee.

✳ *Mathew 11:10*

And as they departed, Jesus began to say unto the multitudes concerning John, What went ye out into the wilderness to see? A reed shaken with the wind? But what went ye out for to see? A man clothed in soft raiment? behold, they that wear soft clothing are in kings' houses. But what went ye out for to see? A prophet? yea, I say unto you, and more than a prophet. For this is he, of whom it is written, Behold, I send my messenger before thy face, which shall prepare thy way before thee. Verily I say unto you,

John the Baptist

Among them that are born of women there hath not risen a greater than John the Baptist: notwithstanding he that is least in the kingdom of heaven is greater than he.

✳ *Mathew 11:7-11*

John began his ministry of baptism of repentance several months prior to his baptism of Jesus, and witnessed the Spirit of the Lord descending upon him.

The next day John seeth Jesus coming unto him, and saith, Behold the Lamb of God, which taketh away the sin of the world. This is he of whom I said, After me cometh a man which is preferred before me: for he was before me. And I knew him not: but that he should be made manifest to Israel, therefore am I come baptizing with water. And John bare record, saying, I saw the Spirit descending from heaven like a dove, and it abode upon him. And I knew him not: but he that sent me to baptize with water, the same said unto me, Upon whom thou shalt see the Spirit descending, and remaining on him, the same is he which baptizeth with the Holy Ghost. And I saw, and bare record that this is the Son of God.

✳ *John 1:29-34*

And the Holy Ghost descended in a bodily shape like a dove upon him, and a voice came from heaven, which said, Thou art my beloved Son; in thee I am well pleased.

✳ *Luke 3:22*

Shortly after Jesus began his ministry, John was imprisoned, and later killed by Herod.

In the New Testament

XV. Son of God, Son of Man

Now when Jesus was born in Bethlehem of Judaea in the days of Herod the king, behold, there came wise men from the east to Jerusalem, Saying, Where is he that is born King of the Jews? for we have seen his star in the east, and are come to worship him.

✳ *Mathew 2:1-2*

The wise men from the East had stopped in Jerusalem to enquire about the birth of Jesus. Herod, surprised to learn this news, asked them where he was to be born.

And when he had gathered all the chief priests and scribes of the people together, he demanded of them where Christ should be born. And they said unto him, In Bethlehem of Judaea: for thus it is written by the prophet,

✳ *Mathew 2:4-5*

Herod tells the wise men to go find out where the child stays and to return with the news so he could worship him also.

When they had heard the king, they departed; and, lo, the star, which they saw in the east, went before them, till it came and stood over where the young child was. When they saw the star, they rejoiced with exceeding great joy. And when they were come into the house, they saw the young child with Mary his mother, and fell down, and worshipped him: and when they had opened their treasures, they presented unto him gifts; gold, and frankincense, and myrrh.

✷ *Mathew 2:9-11*

God warned the wise men in a dream not to return to Herod, so they returned to their country a different route.

And the Angel of the Lord appeared to Joseph in a dream and told him to quickly depart for Egypt and reside there until Herod was dead. And he, Mary and Jesus did reside there until Herod's death. Then God appeared to Joseph in a dream and told him to return to Israel. And they did depart and fulfilled the prophecy;

When Israel was a child, then I loved him, and called my son out of Egypt.

✷ *Hosea 11:1*

Joseph learned that Archelaus, son of Herod was ruler in Judea, and being warned by God in a dream, he went to Galilee instead, to Nazareth, and resided there.

And it is said of Jesus' early years;

And the child grew, and waxed strong in spirit, filled with wisdom: and the grace of God was upon him.

* *Luke 2:40*

When Jesus was 12, he was with his parents Mary and Joseph in Jerusalem at the feast of the passover. And Jesus stayed behind after they had returned home, unbeknownst to them, thinking he was with kin. After 3 days they found him in Jerusalem in the temple hearing and asking questions.

And it came to pass, that after three days they found him in the temple, sitting in the midst of the doctors, both hearing them, and asking them questions. And all that heard him were astonished at his understanding and answers.

* *Luke 2:46-47*

When Mary expresses concern and questions Jesus about it, they did not understand his response.

And when they saw him, they were amazed: and his mother said unto him, Son, why hast thou thus dealt with us? behold, thy father and I have sought thee sorrowing. And he said unto them, How is it that ye sought me? wist ye not that I must be about my Father's business? And they understood not the saying which he spake unto them. And he went down with them, and came to Nazareth, and was subject unto them: but his mother kept all these sayings in her heart. And Jesus increased in wisdom and stature, and in favour with God and man.

* *Luke 2:48-52*

Jesus was around thirty years old when he began his ministry. After his baptism and return from Jordan, he was spirit led into the wilderness where he spent 40 days fasting and facing temptations by the devil, which he resisted. After, he returned to Galilee and taught in synagogues, and in Nazareth, he went on the Sabbath to the synagogue and read, which was usual practice for him.

And there was delivered unto him the book of the prophet Esaias. And when he had opened the book, he found the place where it was written, The Spirit of the Lord is upon me, because he hath anointed me to preach the gospel to the poor; he hath sent me to heal the brokenhearted, to preach deliverance to the captives, and recovering of sight to the blind, to set at liberty them that are bruised, To preach the acceptable year of the Lord.

* *Luke 4:17-19*

And he began to say unto them, This day is this scripture fulfilled in your ears. And all bare him witness, and wondered at the gracious words which proceeded out of his mouth. And they said, Is not this Joseph's son? And he said unto them, Ye will surely say unto me this proverb, Physician, heal thyself: whatsoever we have heard done in Capernaum, do also here in thy country. And he said, Verily I say unto you, No prophet is accepted in his own country. But I tell you of a truth, many widows were in Israel in the days of Elias, when the heaven was shut up three years and six months, when great famine was throughout all the land; But unto none of them was Elias sent, save unto Sarepta, a city of Sidon, unto a woman that was a widow. And many lepers were in Israel in the time of Eliseus the prophet; and none of them was cleansed, saving Naaman the Syrian.

* *Luke 4:21-27*

Jesus references Isaiah's writings and calls out God's favor is not limited to the people of Israel, that his grace and mercy are available to all who believe, in this case Gentiles. This enrages them, and he is driven out of town where he goes to Capernaum.

And after driving out an evil spirit from a man in the synagogue there and healing Simon's mother from a fever, word grew and he healed and drove out evil spirits from many more as they called on him for healing. They asked him to stay with them.

And he said unto them, I must preach the kingdom of God to other cities also: for therefore am I sent. And he preached in the synagogues of Galilee.

* *Luke 4:44*

Jesus chose 12 disciples to teach his message to, which he referred to specifically as his Apostles, who learned from and followed him, and taught others about his message. For a period of around three years, he and they taught and ministered throughout Galilee, Jerusalem and Judea, beyond the Jordan East in Perea and Decapolis and West in Samaria.

Jesus drew the ire of the Jewish scribes and Pharisees, prominent religious leaders of the times. As he continued to heal many, and they saw his following develop, the miracles he performed and the message he preached, this threatened their authority and the interpretations of their laws and they developed plans to entrap him.

They tried to get him to say something they could use against him, and accused him of blasphemy (they rejected his claim of the authority given him from God and that he is the Son of God), and they accused Jesus of doing the work of the devil when he exorcised unclean spirits. Because of their fear of his rising power and following and their jealousy and misunderstanding of his mission, they sought his end and so began events that led to his death.

Many played roles in Jesus' arrest, trial, sentencing and crucifixion. Judas, the disciple who betrayed Jesus for 30 pieces of silver, the current and former high priests Caiaphas and Annas (his father in law, who retained considerable influence), who sought to have Jesus condemned for fear of his growing influence and following, and the Roman Prefect of Judea Pontius Pilot, who caved to pressures and was swayed by the priests and others against Jesus.

God's plan from the beginning was for salvation, since the fall of man and sin upon him had entered the world thousands of years prior in the Garden of Eden. And salvation only by the blood of Christ for his chosen, for those who believe in and follow him.

The events leading to Jesus' condemnation and death, and those involved, were thus part of God's plan.

Then Judas, which had betrayed him, when he saw that he was condemned, repented himself, and brought again the thirty pieces of silver to the chief priests and elders, Saying, I have sinned in that I have betrayed the innocent blood. And they said, What is that to us? see thou to that.

✻ *Mathew 27:3-4*

The Son of man goeth as it is written of him: but woe unto that man by whom the Son of man is betrayed! it had been good for that man if he had not been born.

✻ *Mathew 26:24*

While I was with them in the world, I kept them in thy name:

those that thou gavest me I have kept, and none of them is lost, but the son of perdition; that the scripture might be fulfilled.

✳ *John 17:12*

And Luke writes; *Him, being delivered by the determinate counsel and foreknowledge of God, ye have taken, and by wicked hands have crucified and slain:*

✳ *Acts 2:23*

On the third day after Jesus' death he was resurrected, his tomb empty. Mary Magdalene and the other Mary upon visiting the tomb, were told by the angel that Jesus had risen, to see for themselves, to go tell his disciples, and that Jesus had gone before them to Galilee where they would see him.

Jesus spent 40 days in his resurrected state being witnessed by many, and by over 500 on one occasion. Paul writes;

And that he was buried, and that he rose again the third day according to the scriptures: And that he was seen of Cephas, then of the twelve: After that, he was seen of above five hundred brethren at once; of whom the greater part remain unto this present, but some are fallen asleep. After that, he was seen of James; then of all the apostles. And last of all he was seen of me also, as of one born out of due time.

✳ *1 Corinthians 15:4-8*

Son of God, Son of Man

On the 40th day post-resurrection Jesus led the disciples to Bethany, near the Mount of Olives, and opened his arms and while blessing them, he was taken up into heaven. His ascension marks the completion of his earthly ministry and his complete defeat of the enemy, of death. It signifies Jesus' power, authority and of the Holy Spirit sent to empower and indwell within his followers. Jesus said to his disciples;

And he said unto them, These are the words which I spake unto you, while I was yet with you, that all things must be fulfilled, which were written in the law of Moses, and in the prophets, and in the psalms, concerning me. Then opened he their understanding, that they might understand the scriptures, And said unto them, Thus it is written, and thus it behoved Christ to suffer, and to rise from the dead the third day: And that repentance and remission of sins should be preached in his name among all nations, beginning at Jerusalem. And ye are witnesses of these things. And, behold, I send the promise of my Father upon you: but tarry ye in the city of Jerusalem, until ye be endued with power from on high. And he led them out as far as to Bethany, and he lifted up his hands, and blessed them. And it came to pass, while he blessed them, he was parted from them, and carried up into heaven.

* *Luke 24:44-51*

While Jesus' disciples stood and watched his ascension, an angel of the Lord spoke to them;

And while they looked stedfastly toward heaven as he went up, behold, two men stood by them in white apparel; Which also said, Ye men of Galilee, why stand ye gazing up into heaven? this same Jesus, which is taken up from you into heaven, shall so come in like manner as ye have seen him go into heaven.

✷ *Acts 1:11*

And they worshipped him, and returned to Jerusalem with great joy: And were continually in the temple, praising and blessing God. Amen.

✷ *Luke 24:52-53*

Jesus' Disciples remained in Jerusalem as he'd instructed them prior to his ascension, to await the Holy Spirit sent to them from God, and approximately 10 days later came the day of Pentecost when they were imbued from on high.

And when the day of Pentecost was fully come, they were all with one accord in one place. And suddenly there came a sound from heaven as of a rushing mighty wind, and it filled all the house where they were sitting. And there appeared unto them cloven tongues like as of fire, and it sat upon each of them. And they were all filled with the Holy Ghost, and began to speak with other tongues, as the Spirit gave them utterance.

✷ *Acts 2:1-4*

Son of God, Son of Man

Jesus walked the earth for some 33 years, living a sinless life. The missionary plan of his Gospel message is for his teachings to be spread to every people and nation. He preaches living a life for God different than a life lived of this world. Paul writes;

And be not conformed to this world: but be ye transformed by the renewing of your mind, that ye may prove what is that good, and acceptable, and perfect, will of God.

✳ *Romans 12:2*

We await Jesus' return with eager hearts and souls, our treasures lie in him, that he will establish his Kingdom, the New Jerusalem here on Earth.

XVI. Jesus and his Disciples

Jesus began his ministry after returning from the 40 days he spent in the wilderness. He began preaching the gospel message and healing the sick, blind, lame and raising some from the dead. He gathered disciples that would follow him, and chose the 12 Apostles he taught, ministered and performed miracles with.

And Jesus, walking by the sea of Galilee, saw two brethren, Simon called Peter, and Andrew his brother, casting a net into the sea: for they were fishers. And he saith unto them, Follow me, and I will make you fishers of men. And they straightway left their nets, and followed him. And going on from thence, he saw other two brethren, James the son of Zebedee, and John his brother, in a ship with Zebedee their father, mending their nets; and he called them. And they immediately left the ship and their father, and followed him.

✷ *Mathew 4:18-22*

And when a crowd gathered to hear him and was too many, Jesus and his disciples departed in the boat. While at sea, a storm came about and his disciples feared for their lives. They sought Jesus and found him asleep.

And his disciples came to him, and awoke him, saying, Lord, save us: we perish. And he saith unto them, Why are ye fearful, O ye of little faith? Then he arose, and rebuked the winds and the sea; and there was a great calm. But the men marvelled, saying, What manner of man is this, that even the winds and the sea obey him!

✳ *Mathew 8:25-27*

When Jesus saw so many that gathered to hear him and to be healed, he was moved.

Then saith he unto his disciples, The harvest truly is plenteous, but the labourers are few; Pray ye therefore the Lord of the harvest, that he will send forth labourers into his harvest.

✳ *Mathew 9:37-38*

When Jesus had chosen his 12 Apostles, he gave them power to perform miracles of healing and commanded of them many things.

And when he had called unto him his twelve disciples, he gave them power against unclean spirits, to cast them out, and to heal all manner of sickness and all manner of disease. Now the names of the twelve apostles are these; The first, Simon, who is called Peter, and Andrew his brother; James the son of Zebedee, and John his brother; Philip, and Bartholomew; Thomas, and Matthew the publican; James the son of Alphaeus, and Lebbaeus, whose surname was Thaddaeus; Simon the Canaanite, and Judas Iscariot, who also betrayed him.

✳ *Mathew 10:1-4*

And as ye go, preach, saying, The kingdom of heaven is at hand. Heal the sick, cleanse the lepers, raise the dead, cast out devils: freely ye have received, freely give.

✳ *Mathew 10:7-8*

Behold, I send you forth as sheep in the midst of wolves: be ye therefore wise as serpents, and harmless as doves. But beware of men: for they will deliver you up to the councils, and they will scourge you in their synagogues;

✳ *Mathew 10:16-17*

And ye shall be hated of all men for my name's sake: but he that endureth to the end shall be saved.

✳ *Mathew 10:22*

Whosoever therefore shall confess me before men, him will I confess also before my Father which is in heaven. But whosoever shall deny me before man, him will I also deny before my Father which is in heaven.

✳ *Mathew 10:32-33*

Jesus and his Disciples

After hearing that John the Baptist had been killed by Herod, Jesus goes with his disciples by boat to a desert place outside the city. When news of his arrival spreads, many come to see and hear him, and he performs a miracle feeding of 5000 with 5 loaves of bread and 2 fish.

And Jesus went forth, and saw a great multitude, and was moved with compassion toward them, and he healed their sick. And when it was evening, his disciples came to him, saying, This is a desert place, and the time is now past; send the multitude away, that they may go into the villages, and buy themselves victuals. But Jesus said unto them, They need not depart; give ye them to eat. And they say unto him, We have here but five loaves, and two fishes.

* *Mathew 14:14-17*

He said, Bring them hither to me. And he commanded the multitude to sit down on the grass, and took the five loaves, and the two fishes, and looking up to heaven, he blessed, and brake, and gave the loaves to his disciples, and the disciples to the multitude. And they did all eat, and were filled: and they took up of the fragments that remained twelve baskets full. And they that had eaten were about five thousand men, beside women and children.

* *Mathew 14:18-21*

After departing from there by boat, a storm arose while they

were on the sea, and in its midst Jesus' disciples saw him out walking on the water, and they were afraid.

And when the disciples saw him walking on the sea, they were troubled, saying, It is a spirit; and they cried out for fear. But straightway Jesus spake unto them, saying, Be of good cheer; it is I; be not afraid. And Peter answered him and said, Lord, if it be thou, bid me come unto thee on the water. And he said, Come. And when Peter was come down out of the ship, he walked on the water, to go to Jesus. But when he saw the wind boisterous, he was afraid; and beginning to sink, he cried, saying, Lord, save me. And immediately Jesus stretched forth his hand, and caught him, and said unto him, O thou of little faith, wherefore didst thou doubt? And when they were come into the ship, the wind ceased. Then they that were in the ship came and worshipped him, saying, Of a truth thou art the Son of God.

✱ *Mathew 14:26-33*

Jesus asked his disciples who the people say who he is.

When Jesus came into the coasts of Caesarea Philippi, he asked his disciples, saying, Whom do men say that I the Son of man am? And they said, Some say that thou art John the Baptist: some, Elias; and others, Jeremiah, or one of the prophets. He saith unto them, But whom say ye that I am? And Simon Peter answered and said, Thou art the Christ, the Son of the living God. And Jesus answered and said unto him, Blessed art thou, Simon Bar-jona:

for flesh and blood hath not revealed it unto thee, but my Father which is in heaven. And I say also unto thee, That thou art Peter, and upon this rock I will build my church; and the gates of hell shall not prevail against it. And I will give unto thee the keys of the kingdom of heaven: and whatsoever thou shalt bind on earth shall be bound in heaven: and whatsoever thou shalt loose on earth shall be loosed in heaven.

✶ *Mathew 16:13-19*

From that time forth began Jesus to shew unto his disciples, how that he must go unto Jerusalem, and suffer many things of the elders and chief priests and scribes, and be killed, and be raised again the third day.

✶ *Mathew 16:21*

Disciples Peter, James and John, who were with Jesus, saw his Transfiguration on the Mount, and God Spoke.

And as he prayed, the fashion of his countenance was altered, and his raiment was white and glistering. And, behold, there talked with him two men, which were Moses and Elias: Who appeared in glory, and spake of his decease which he should accomplish at Jerusalem.

✶ *Luke 9:29-30*

And there came a voice out of the cloud, saying, This is my beloved Son: hear him.

* *Luke 9:35*

Soon after, Jesus entered Jerusalem with his disciples, which then began events that would culminate in his sentencing and crucifixion later that week. He rode in on a donkey, fulfilling the Old Testament prophecy from Zechariah 9:9, to a crowd praising him as Messiah. In the synagogue, he overturned tables of the moneychangers who were conducting business there. In the temple, Jesus' teachings are questioned by the chief priests, Pharisees and Sadducees. He speaks to them in parables and warns them of the things to come and the consequences of their ways. They conspired against him.

Then assembled together the chief priests, and the scribes, and the elders of the people, unto the palace of the high priest, who was called Caiaphas, And consulted that they might take Jesus by subtilty, and kill him.

* *Mathew 26:3-4*

Peter, James, John and Andrew accompany Jesus to the Mount of Olives where he teaches them of things to come and to be prepared for his return, his second coming.

And it came to pass, when Jesus had finished all these sayings, he said unto his disciples, Ye know that after two days is the feast of the passover, and the Son of man is betrayed to be crucified.

✳ *Mathew 26:1-2*

Jesus gives his disciples instructions to prepare for the last supper. He washes their feet, and calls out Judas Iscariot as the disciple who would betray him. Later that evening Jesus is arrested in the Garden of Gethsemane. He is sentenced to death and crucified.

After Jesus' resurrection, he appears to his disciples, spends time with them and among many of the conversations he has with them prior to his ascension he says;

And that repentance and remission of sins should be preached in his name among all nations, beginning at Jerusalem. And ye are witnesses of these things.

✳ *Luke 24:47-48*

XVII. The Apostle Paul

Paul, known prior to his conversion to Christianity as Saul, and Saul of Tarsus, was a persecutor of early Christians. He was a strict follower of Pharisaic Judaism, and a zealot for the traditions and laws of his Jewish faith. He viewed early followers of Jesus as a threat to his religion and sought to silence them. He was present at and consenting to the stoning of Stephen, the first Christian martyr.

Paul is confronted on the Road to Damascus, encountering a bright light from Heaven and is spoken to by Jesus.

And Saul, yet breathing out threatenings and slaughter against the disciples of the Lord, went unto the high priest, And desired of him letters to Damascus to the synagogues, that if he found any of this way, whether they were men or women, he might bring them bound unto Jerusalem. And as he journeyed, he came near Damascus: and suddenly there shined round about him a light from heaven: And he fell to the earth, and heard a voice saying unto him, Saul, Saul, why persecutest thou me? And he said, Who art thou, Lord? And the Lord said, I am Jesus whom thou persecutest:...

✳ *Acts 9:1-5*

Jesus spoke to Paul of what he wanted him to do.

But rise, and stand upon thy feet: for I have appeared unto thee

for this purpose, to make thee a minister and a witness both of these things which thou hast seen, and of those things in the which I will appear unto thee; Delivering thee from the people, and from the Gentiles, unto whom now I send thee, To open their eyes, and to turn them from darkness to light, and from the power of Satan unto God, that they may receive forgiveness of sins, and inheritance among them which are sanctified by faith that is in me.

✳ *Acts 26:16-18*

Paul is told by Jesus to continue on to the city where he'd be instructed further.

For three days he was without sight, food or drink. While in Damascus, he was visited by Ananias who'd received in a vision instructions from the Lord.

And Ananias went his way, and entered into the house; and putting his hands on him said, Brother Saul, the Lord, even Jesus, that appeared unto thee in the way as thou camest, hath sent me, that thou mightest receive thy sight, and be filled with the Holy Ghost. And immediately there fell from his eyes as it had been scales: and he received sight forthwith, and arose, and was baptized. And when he had received meat, he was strengthened. Then was Saul certain days with the disciples which were at Damascus.

✳ *Acts 9:27-30*

Paul's ministry and work for the faith was prolific, spreading the Gospel message of the risen Christ throughout Asia Minor, on missionary journeys to, and establishing churches in Ephesus, Philippi, Thessalonica, Corinth, and Galatia. He was imprisoned by the Romans for his faith and eventually martyred. He wrote nearly half the books in the New Testament.

Paul writes to Timothy from prison when his time is near to being glorified, having kept the faith to the end.

For I am now ready to be offered, and the time of my departure is at hand. I have fought a good fight, I have finished my course, I have kept the faith: Henceforth there is laid up for me a crown of righteousness, which the Lord, the righteous judge, shall give me at that day: and not to me only, but unto all them also that love his appearing.

✳ *2 Timothy 4:6-8*

XVIII. By God's Grace Alone Are We Saved

The Apostle Paul writes that we are all sinners and in need of redemption through Christ;

For all have sinned, and come short of the glory of God; Being justified freely by his grace through the redemption that is in Christ Jesus: Whom God hath set forth to be a propitiation through faith in his blood, to declare his righteousness for the remission of sins that are past, through the forbearance of God;

✳ *Romans 3:23-25*

He writes; *But God commendeth his love toward us, in that, while we were yet sinners, Christ died for us.*

✳ *Romans 5:8*

Christianity is not "works based" salvation. It is by God's grace alone that we are saved, we do nothing to earn our salvation.

Paul writes: *For by grace are ye saved through faith; and that not of yourselves: it is the gift of God: Not of works, lest any man should boast.*

✳ *Ephesians 2:8-9*

XIX. Being a Follower of Christ

Jesus says; *I am the light of the world: he that followeth me shall not walk in darkness, but shall have the light of life.*

✳ *John 8:12*

Being a follower of Jesus Christ is to believe in God's plan of salvation, as revealed in the Gospels, that Jesus his son was conceived by the Holy Spirit, born of the Virgin Mary, was crucified and died on the cross, that on the 3rd day following he rose from the dead, and ascended into Heaven after revealing to many his resurrected self.

As a believer in and follower of Jesus, our sin no longer keeps us from God, as Christ's atonement for our sin has righted us in his eyes. This is fulfillment of prophecy and testament to God's redemptive plan for us, from which we are justified and made righteous to him.

Jesus says; *I am the way, and the truth, and the life. No one comes to the Father except through me.*

✳ *John 14:6*

XX. God's Gift of Eternal Life with Him

Eternal salvation is the gift given from God to us who believe in and follow Jesus.

Jesus says: *I am the resurrection and the life: he that believeth in me, though he were dead, yet shall he live:*

✳ *John 11:25*

Paul writes: *For the wages of sin is death; but the gift of God is eternal life through Jesus Christ our Lord.*

✳ *Romans 6:23*

XXI. Repentance, God's Forgiveness, Forgiving Others

Wash me thoroughly from mine iniquity, and cleanse me from my sin. For I acknowledge my transgressions: and my sin is ever before me.

* *Psalm 51:2-3*

As sinners, we confess and repent of our sins to God, and ask for forgiveness in his son Jesus.

But if we walk in the light, as he is in the light, we have fellowship one with another, and the blood of Jesus Christ his Son cleanseth us from all sin. If we say that we have no sin, we deceive ourselves, and the truth is not in us. If we confess our sins, he is faithful and just to forgive us our sins, and to cleanse us from all unrighteousness.

* *1 John 1:7-9*

And having forgiveness for our sins from our Father in Heaven, we are to forgive others.

For if ye forgive men their trespasses, your heavenly Father will also forgive you: But if ye forgive not men their trespasses, neither will your Father forgive your trespasses.

* *Mathew 6:14-15*

The Holy Spirit

XXII. Sealed by the Spirit

Paul writes; *In whom ye also trusted, after that ye heard the word of truth, the gospel of your salvation: in whom also after that ye believed, ye were sealed with that holy Spirit of promise,*

✴ *Ephesians 1:13*

Upon accepting Christ as our Savior, we are sent the Holy Spirit, the 3rd person of the Godhead, the Spirit of Truth, our Comforter to dwell within us. We are thus "Born Again", given the gift of eternal life, and become part of the collective Body of Christ, his elect.

In speaking with Nicodemus; *Jesus answered, Verily, verily, I say unto thee, Except a man be born of water and of the Spirit, he cannot enter into the kingdom of God. That which is born of the flesh is flesh; and that which is born of the Spirit is spirit. Marvel not that I said unto thee, Ye must be born again.*

✴ *John 3:5-7*

Jesus says; *And I will pray the Father, and he shall give you another Comforter, that he may abide with you for ever; Even the Spirit of truth; whom the world cannot receive, because it seeth him not, neither knoweth him: but ye know him; for he dwelleth with you, and shall be in you. I will not leave you comfortless: I* will come to you.

✳ *John 14:16-18*

Jesus says; *But the Comforter, which is the Holy Ghost, whom the Father will send in my name, he shall teach you all things, and bring all things to your remembrance, whatsoever I have said unto you.*

✳ *John 14:26*

Paul writes; *The Spirit itself beareth witness with our spirit, that we are the children of God:*

✳ *Romans 8:16*

XXIII. Empowered with the Spirit

Paul writes; *But if the Spirit of him that raised up Jesus from the dead dwell in you, he that raised up Christ from the dead shall also quicken your mortal bodies by his Spirit that dwelleth in you.*

✳ *Romans 8:11*

And Paul writes; *For this cause I bow my knees unto the Father of our Lord Jesus Christ, of whom the whole family in heaven and earth is named, that he would grant you, according to the riches of his glory, to be strengthened with might by his Spirit in the inner man; that Christ may dwell in your hearts by faith; that ye, being rooted and grounded in love, may be able to comprehend with all saints what is the breadth, and length, and depth, and height; and to know the love of Christ, which passeth knowledge, that ye might be filled with all the fulness of God. Now unto him that is able to do exceeding abundantly above all that we ask or think, according to the power that worketh in us, unto him be glory in the church by Christ Jesus throughout all ages, world without end. Amen.*

✳ *Ephesians 3:14-21*

Paul writes; *For God hath not given us the spirit of fear; but of power, and of love, and of a sound mind.*

✳ *2 Timothy 1:7*

Jesus says; *But ye shall receive power, after that the Holy Ghost is come upon you: and ye shall be witnesses unto me both in Jerusalem, and in all Judaea, and in Samaria, and unto the uttermost part of the earth.*

✳ *Acts 1:8*

John writes; *Ye are of God, little children, and have overcome them: because greater is he that is in you, than he that is in the world.*

✳ *1 John 4:4*

The Holy Spirit empowers us to use scripture as a weapon in spiritual battles.

Paul writes: *And take the helmet of salvation, and the sword of the Spirit, which is the word of God:*

✳ *Ephesians 6:17*

XXIV. The Holy Spirit's Work in Us

From our relationship with Christ and the Holy Spirit's work within us we develop the fruits of the Spirit: love, joy, peace, patience, kindness, faithfulness, goodness, gentleness, and self-control.

But the fruit of the Spirit is love, joy, peace, longsuffering, gentleness, goodness, faith, meekness, temperance: against such there is no law.

✳ *Galatians 5:22-23*

We are humble in our spirit, so the presence of the Holy Spirit in us is forefront. The Holy Spirit sanctifies us, transforming us to be more Christlike.

But we all, with open face beholding as in a glass the glory of the Lord, are changed into the same image from glory to glory, even as by the Spirit of the Lord.

✳ *2 Corinthians 3:18*

The Holy Spirit works in us to the will of God and guides us in the truth.

Paul writes; *For it is God which worketh in you both to will and to do of his good pleasure.*

✳ *Philippians 2:13*

Jesus says; *Howbeit when he, the Spirit of truth, is come, he will guide you into all truth: for he shall not speak of himself; but whatsoever he shall hear, that shall he speak: and he will shew you things to come.*

✳ *John 16:13*

Obedience, God's Divinity and Power

XXV. Following God's Law

Soon after the Exodus of the Israelites from Egypt, God spoke to them the ten commandments at Mount Sinai.

And God spake all these words, saying, I am the LORD thy God, which have brought thee out of the land of Egypt, out of the house of bondage.

Thou shalt have no other gods before me.

Thou shalt not make unto thee any graven image, or any likeness of any thing that is in heaven above, or that is in the earth beneath, or that is in the water under the earth: thou shalt not bow down thyself to them, nor serve them: for I the LORD thy God am a jealous God, visiting the iniquity of the fathers upon the children unto the third and fourth generation of them that hate me; and shewing mercy unto thousands of them that love me, and keep my commandments.

Thou shalt not take the name of the LORD thy God in vain; for the LORD will not hold him guiltless that taketh his name in vain.

Remember the sabbath day, to keep it holy. Six days shalt thou labour, and do all thy work: but the seventh day is the sabbath of the LORD thy God: in it thou shalt not do any work, thou, nor thy son, nor thy daughter, thy manservant, nor thy maidservant, nor thy cattle, nor thy stranger that is within thy gates: for in six days the LORD made heaven and earth, the sea, and all that in them is, and rested the seventh day: wherefore the LORD blessed the sabbath day, and hallowed it.

Honour thy father and thy mother: that thy days may be long upon the land which the LORD thy God giveth thee.
Thou shalt not kill.
Thou shalt not commit adultery.
Thou shalt not steal.
Thou shalt not bear false witness against thy neighbour.
Thou shalt not covet thy neighbour's house, thou shalt not covet thy neighbour's wife, nor his manservant, nor his maidservant, nor his ox, nor his ass, nor any thing that is thy neighbour's.

✳ *Exodus 20:1-17*

Regarding the 4th commandment, which is different from the moral law commandments, Jesus says and demonstrated that such rigid interpretation of and restrictions concerning the Mosaic Sabbath (Saturday) would no longer be upheld or required. In the New Covenant in Christ, regarding the rest it concerns, important for us now is salvation rest, that comes from our faith in God. And a particular day is not of concern. Observance is Sunday, the day change (to Sunday) not a commandment, but Church tradition to this day.

And he said unto them, The sabbath was made for man, and not man for the sabbath: therefore the Son of man is Lord also of the sabbath.

* Mark 2:27-28

Let no man therefore judge you in meat, or in drink, or in respect of an holyday, or of the new moon, or of the sabbath days: which are a shadow of things to come; but the body is of Christ.

* Colossians 2:16-17

And in keeping the moral commandments, we demonstrate our love for God and desire to be like him.

What then? shall we sin, because we are not under the law, but under grace? God forbid.

* Romans 6:14

For verily I say unto you, Till heaven and earth pass, one jot or one tittle shall in no wise pass from the law, till all be fulfilled.

* Mathew 5:18

Do we then make void the law through faith? God forbid: yea, we establish the law.

* Romans 3:31

XXVI. Rewards of Obedience

And all these blessings shall come on thee, and overtake thee, if thou shalt hearken unto the voice of the LORD thy God.

✳ *Deuteronomy 28:2*

Acquaint now thyself with him, and be at peace: thereby good shall come unto thee. Receive, I pray thee, the law from his mouth, and lay up his words in thine heart. If thou return to the Almighty, thou shalt be built up, thou shalt put away iniquity far from thy tabernacles.

✳ *Job 22:21-23*

The law of the LORD is perfect, converting the soul: the testimony of the LORD is sure, making wise the simple. The statutes of the LORD are right, rejoicing the heart: the commandment of the LORD is pure, enlightening the eyes. The fear of the LORD is clean, enduring for ever: the judgments of the LORD are true and righteous altogether. More to be desired are they than gold, yea, than much fine gold: sweeter also than honey and the honeycomb. Moreover by them is thy servant warned: and in keeping of them there is great reward.

✳ *Psalm 19:7-11*

XXVII. God's Divinity and Power

Hast thou not known? hast thou not heard, that the everlasting God, the LORD, the Creator of the ends of the earth, fainteth not, neither is weary? there is no searching of his understanding. He giveth power to the faint; and to them that have no might he increaseth strength.

✴ *Isaiah 40:28-29*

Peter writes; *According as his divine power hath given unto us all things that pertain unto life and godliness, through the knowledge of him that hath called us to glory and virtue: whereby are given unto us exceeding great and precious promises: that by these ye might be partakers of the divine nature, having escaped the corruption that is in the world through lust.*

✴ *2 Peter 1:3-4*

Paul writes; *For the preaching of the cross is to them that perish foolishness; but unto us which are saved it is the power of God.*

✴ *1 Corinthians 1:18*

Paul writes; *Finally, my brethren, be strong in the Lord, and in the power of his might. Put on the whole armour of God, that ye may be able to stand against the wiles of the devil. For we wrestle not against flesh and blood, but against principalities, against powers, against the rulers of the darkness of this world, against spiritual wickedness in high places. Wherefore take unto you the whole armour of God, that ye may be able to withstand in the evil day, and having done all, to stand.*

✱ *Ephesians 6:10-13*

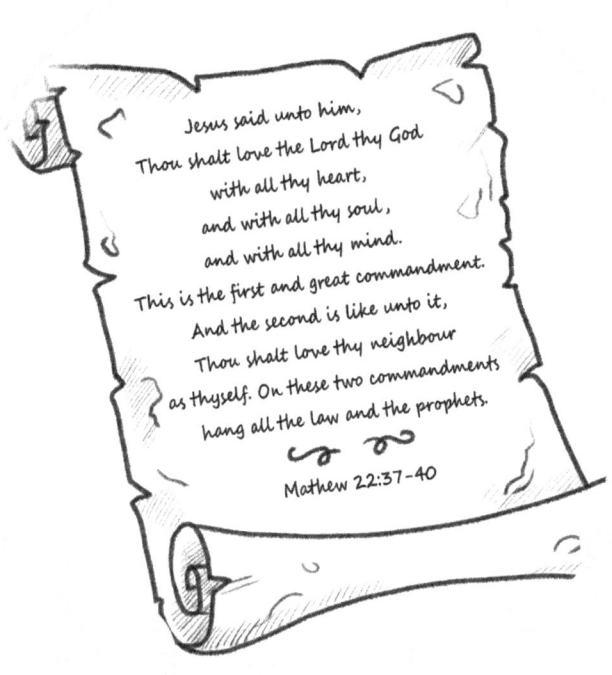

Jesus said unto him,
Thou shalt love the Lord thy God
with all thy heart,
and with all thy soul,
and with all thy mind.
This is the first and great commandment.
And the second is like unto it,
Thou shalt love thy neighbour
as thyself. On these two commandments
hang all the law and the prophets.

Mathew 22:37-40

Love Abounds in God

XXVIII. Love God, Love Others, God's Love

Jesus said unto him, *Thou shalt love the Lord thy God with all thy heart, and with all thy soul, and with all thy mind. This is the first and great commandment. And the second is like unto it, Thou shalt love thy neighbour as thyself. On these two commandments hang all the law and the prophets.*

✳ *Mathew 22:37-40*

Jesus says; *If ye love me, keep my commandments.*

✳ *John 14:15*

John writes: *For this is the love of God, that we keep his commandments: and his commandments are not grievous.*

✳ *1 John 5:3*

He writes; *Beloved, let us love one another: for love is of God; and every one that loveth is born of God, and knoweth God. He that loveth not knoweth not God; for God is love.*

✳ *1 John 4:7-8*

Peter writes; *Seeing ye have purified your souls in obeying the truth through the Spirit unto unfeigned love of the brethren, see that ye love one another with a pure heart fervently:*

* *1 Peter 1:22*

Paul writes; *For I am persuaded, that neither death, nor life, nor angels, nor principalities, nor powers, nor things present, nor things to come, Nor height, nor depth, nor any other creature, shall be able to separate us from the love of God, which is in Christ Jesus our Lord.*

* *Romans 8:38*

Jesus says; *For God so loved the world, that he gave his only Son, that whoever believes in him should not perish but have eternal life.*

* *John 3:16*

XXIX. Serving and Spreading the Word

Abiding in and following Jesus involves spreading the Gospel message to others.

Jesus says; *I am the vine, ye are the branches: He that abideth in me, and I in him, the same bringeth forth much fruit: for without me ye can do nothing.*

∗ *John 15:5*

Paul writes; *For we are his workmanship, created in Christ Jesus to do good works, which God prepared beforehand for us to do.*

∗ *Ephesians 2:10*

He writes; *And whatsoever ye do in word or deed, do all in the name of the Lord Jesus, giving thanks to God and the Father by him.*

∗ *Colossians 3:17*

Jesus tells his disciples; *Go therefore and make disciples of all the nations, baptizing them in the name of the Father and of the Son and of the Holy Spirit.*

∗ *Mathew 28:16*

Mary Magdalene and the other Mary mentioned in scripture accompanying her, upon visiting the tomb where Jesus was kept following his death, encounter an angel.

Mathew writes; *And the angel answered and said unto the women, Fear not ye: for I know that ye seek Jesus, which was crucified. He is not here: for he is risen, as he said. Come, see the place where the Lord lay. And go quickly, and tell his disciples that he is risen from the dead; and, behold, he goeth before you into Galilee; there shall ye see him: lo, I have told you.*

✳ *Mathew 28:5-7*

Paul writes; *Let a man so account of us, as of the ministers of Christ, and stewards of the mysteries of God.*

✳ *1 Corinthians 4:1*

We are to contend for the faith, spreading the message of Jesus Christ and him crucified, maintaining the sanctity of his teachings, not taking from or adding to them in any way.

But though we, or an angel from heaven, preach any other gospel unto you than that which we have preached unto you, let him be accursed.

✳ *Galatians 1:8*

XXX. Treasures Await in the Lord

Our treasures in life lie not in earthly things, but in gifts and blessings we receive from above in following Christ and being obedient to the word of God.

Jesus says; *For where your treasure is, there will your heart be also.*

✳ *Mathew 6:21*

Paul writes; *Set your affection on things above, not on things on the earth.*

✳ *Colossians 3:2*

And he writes about God; *In whom are hid all the treasures of wisdom and knowledge.*

✳ *Colossians 2:3*

Jesus says; *Ask, and it shall be given you; seek, and ye shall find; knock, and it shall be opened unto you:*

✳ *Matthew 7:7*

And Paul writes; *But of him are ye in Christ Jesus, who of God is made unto us wisdom, and righteousness, and sanctification, and redemption:*

✳ *1 Corinthians 1:30*

And he writes; *Therefore if any man be in Christ, he is a new creature: old things are passed away; behold, all things are become new.*

✳ *2 Corinthians 5:17*

Have faith in Jesus and God's plan for you. Make Jesus your Lord and Savior and he'll change your life forever. When you are his, he will never leave you.

Jesus says; *And this is the Father's will which hath sent me, that of all which he hath given me I should lose nothing, but should raise it up again at the last day.*

✳ *John 6:39*

Without salvation in Christ, all the treasures in the world amount to nothing.

Jesus says; *For what shall it profit a man, if he shall gain the whole world, and lose his own soul?*

✳ *Mark 8:36*

Prophecy and His Kingdom Come

XXXI. Sign of the Times

Warnings to be discerning, and not to be deceived, and to be watchful and ready were given by Jesus to his followers and by the Apostles to the Church, the Body of Christ.

John writes; *Beloved, believe not every spirit, but try the spirits whether they are of God: because many false prophets are gone out into the world.*

* *1 John 4:1*

Mathew writes; *And Jesus answered and said unto them, Take heed that no man deceive you. For many shall come in my name, saying, I am Christ; and shall deceive many.*

* *Mathew 24:4-5*

Jesus says; *For there shall arise false Christs, and false prophets, and shall shew great signs and wonders; insomuch that, if it were possible, they shall deceive the very elect.*

* *Mathew 24:24*

We are to be watchful and ready.

Paul writes; *For yourselves know perfectly that the day of the*

Lord so cometh as a thief in the night.

✳ *1 Thessalonians 5:2*

Peter writes; *Be sober, be vigilant; because your adversary the devil, as a roaring lion, walketh about, seeking whom he may devour:*

✳ *1 Peter 5:8*

XXXII. Final Events & Christ's Return

Paul writes; *Behold, I shew you a mystery; We shall not all sleep, but we shall all be changed, In a moment, in the twinkling of an eye, at the last trump: for the trumpet shall sound, and the dead shall be raised incorruptible, and we shall be changed.*

✱ *1 Corinthians 15:51-52*

He writes; *For the Lord himself shall descend from heaven with a shout, with the voice of the archangel, and with the trump of God: and the dead in Christ shall rise first: Then we which are alive and remain shall be caught up together with them in the clouds, to meet the Lord in the air: and so shall we ever be with the Lord.*

✱ *1 Thessalonians 4:16-17*

Jesus says; *Immediately after the tribulation of those days shall the sun be darkened, and the moon shall not give her light, and the stars shall fall from heaven, and the powers of the heavens shall be shaken: And then shall appear the sign of the Son of man in heaven: and then shall all the tribes of the earth mourn, and they shall see the Son of man coming in the clouds of heaven with power and great glory. And he shall send his angels with a great sound of a trumpet, and they shall gather together his elect from the four winds, from one end of heaven to the other.*

✱ *Mathew 24:29-31*

And the seventh angel sounded; and there were great voices in heaven, saying, The kingdoms of this world are become the kingdoms of our Lord, and of his Christ; and he shall reign for ever and ever.

✶ *Revelation 11:15*

John writes: *And I John saw the holy city, new Jerusalem, coming down from God out of heaven, prepared as a bride adorned for her husband.*

✶ *Revelation 21:2*

XXXIII. Be Part of His Eternal Kingdom

It is written; *But ye are come unto mount Sion, and unto the city of the living God, the heavenly Jerusalem, and to an innumerable company of angels, To the general assembly and church of the firstborn, which are written in heaven, and to God the Judge of all, and to the spirits of just men made perfect, And to Jesus the mediator of the new covenant, and to the blood of sprinkling, that speaketh better things than that of Abel.*

✳ *Hebrews 12:22-24*

A Psalm or Song for the sons of Korah. His foundation is in the holy mountains. The LORD loveth the gates of Zion more than all the dwellings of Jacob. Glorious things are spoken of thee, O city of God. Selah. I will make mention of Rahab and Babylon to them that know me: Behold Philistia, and Tyre, with Ethiopia; This man was born there. And of Zion it shall be said, This and that man was born in her: And the highest himself shall establish her. The LORD shall count, when he writeth up the people, That this man was born there. Selah. As well the singers as the players on instruments shall be there: All my springs are in thee.

✳ *Psalm 87:1-7*

God's sovereignty reigns supreme over all of our lives. Come to Jesus and be given the gift of eternal life, his Kingdom now and forever.

Daily Guidance & Prayer

XXXIV. Reading the Bible

Read the Bible daily as your guide to the truth of God, it is his living word.

Paul writes; *All scripture is given by inspiration of God, and is profitable for doctrine, for reproof, for correction, for instruction in righteousness:*

✳ *2 Timothy 3:16*

The Bible is the only book that contains the mind of God, the state of man, the way of salvation, the doom of sinners, the happiness of the believer. Read it and be wise, believe it and be saved, practice it and be holy. It is the traveler's map, the pilgrim's staff, the pilot's compass, and the soldier's sword. Read it slowly, read it frequently and read it prayerfully.

✳ *Unknown Author*

XXXV. Prayers for Blessing and Salvation

Heavenly Father we pray for your blessing, that you open our spiritual eyes and ears and help us see and hear your transformative plan for us.

And for all those who do not know you yet, and them who have not yet made your son Jesus their personal Lord and Savior, that they be drawn to you and shown your grace and glory, and the joy, peace and love you provide to those in your kingdom.

Help us realize that you provide for all our needs. We open ourselves to your presence in all areas of our lives. We are made better with your guidance in all we do. Your will, your way, your word and your wisdom we cherish. Be with us now and forever, and help us keep Jesus first and foremost in our lives. We pray this prayer in the name of the Father, Son and Holy Spirit, Amen.

AN INDIVIDUAL PRAYER FOR SALVATION IN CHRIST

Father I confess to you that I am a sinner. I repent of my sins and ask for your forgiveness. I believe that Jesus is your son and that he died on the cross to forgive me of my sins. I believe he was resurrected on the 3rd day. I believe he ascended into heaven. I pray Jesus that you come in to my heart and be my Lord and Savior now and forever. I pray the Holy Spirit be sent to indwell in me, so I am born again. I thank you Lord for your gift of eternal life. Amen

Epilogue

Hardships endured for those called to faith, in both the Old and New Testaments. And likewise, they endure today for followers of Christ.

Being called to faith means carrying on amidst opposition and adversity, knowing the hardship experienced is nothing compared to what is gained being members of God's eternal kingdom.

Confirming the souls of the disciples, and exhorting them to continue in the faith, and that we must through much tribulation enter into the kingdom of God.

✳ *Acts 14:22*

And if children, then heirs; heirs of God, and joint-heirs with Christ; if so be that we suffer with him, that we may be also glorified together. For I reckon that the sufferings of this present time are not worthy to be compared with the glory which shall be revealed in us.

✳ *Romans 8:17-18*

Who shall separate us from the love of Christ? shall tribulation, or distress, or persecution, or famine, or nakedness, or peril, or sword? As it is written, For thy sake we are killed all the day long;

we are accounted as sheep for the slaughter. Nay, in all these things we are more than conquerors through him that loved us.

✳ *Romans 8:35-37*

Beloved, think it not strange concerning the fiery trial which is to try you, as though some strange thing happened unto you: But rejoice, inasmuch as ye are partakers of Christ's sufferings; that, when his glory shall be revealed, ye may be glad also with exceeding joy. If ye be reproached for the name of Christ, happy are ye; for the spirit of glory and of God resteth upon you: on their part he is evil spoken of, but on your part he is glorified.

✳ *1 Peter 4:12-14*

And what shall I more say? for the time would fail me to tell of Gedeon, and of Barak, and of Samson, and of Jephthae; of David also, and Samuel, and of the prophets: Who through faith subdued kingdoms, wrought righteousness, obtained promises, stopped the mouths of lions, Quenched the violence of fire, escaped the edge of the sword, out of weakness were made strong, waxed valiant in fight, turned to flight the armies of the aliens. Women received their dead raised to life again: and others were tortured, not accepting deliverance; that they might obtain a better resurrection: And others had trial of cruel mockings and scourgings, yea, moreover of bonds and imprisonment: They were stoned, they were sawn asunder, were tempted, were slain with the sword: they wandered about in sheepskins and goatskins; being destitute, afflicted, tormented; (Of whom the world was not worthy:) they wandered in deserts, and in mountains, and in dens and caves of the earth. And these all, having obtained a good report through faith, received not the promise: God having provided some better thing for us, that they without us should not be made perfect.

✳ *Hebrews 11:32-40*

About the Author

My journey of faith began again close to a decade ago now, from an origin too long before for me to remember who God is. A seed had been planted early, but never grew and bore fruit.

Fast forward to the writing of this book.

I hadn't planned to write it. I'd been experiencing a nudging though, an urge to spread God's word, and the Gospel message of Jesus, what we in faith are called to do. I want to let others know of this gift of him, in whom I've grown and developed so much through years of study, worship and praise.

About the Illustrator

While working on this book, I had a special gift - the opportunity to embody spiritual texts in images. This project became not only a creative task for me, but also a source of support during a difficult period in my life. While drawing the illustrations, I found peace, inspiration, and new strength.

I believe that these pages will preserve a part of the bright hope that I felt while working on them.

Contact:

calledtofaith.com
info@calledtofaith.com